THE BULL RUN

How Bitcoin Shattered Assumptions,
Reshaped Finance And The
Supply-Demand Dynamics Driving Prices
Sky-High.

Saulsberry Shain

Table of contents

Chapter 1: Introduction

The cryptocurrency market has defied conventional wisdom and staged a remarkable comeback, capturing the attention of investors and market analysts alike. In a landscape dominated by high interest rates and persistent inflationary pressures, the resurgence of cryptocurrencies, particularly Bitcoin, has been nothing short of remarkable.

As central banks around the world grappled with soaring inflation, they embarked on an aggressive monetary tightening path, raising interest rates to levels not seen in decades. Conventional economic theory dictated that such an environment would be detrimental to risk-on assets like cryptocurrencies, which had previously thrived in an era of low interest rates and ample liquidity.

However, the crypto market has proven its resilience, shrugging off the high-interest rate environment and staging a remarkable rally. Bitcoin, the pioneering and most prominent cryptocurrency, has led the charge, breaching the $66,000 mark and inching closer to it's all-time high of $69,000, a level last seen during the halcyon days of near-zero interest rates and the non-fungible token (NFT) craze.

This resurgence has left many market participants scratching their heads, wondering how an asset class once considered a speculative fad could defy the gravitational pull of tighter monetary conditions. The answer lies in a potent cocktail of supply-demand dynamics, institutional adoption, and a growing recognition of cryptocurrencies as a legitimate asset class.

At the heart of this crypto renaissance is a supply-demand imbalance that has tilted the scales in favor of higher prices. On the supply side, the impending "halving" event for Bitcoin, which occurs approximately every four years, is set to reduce the rate at which new bitcoins enter the market by half. This supply squeeze coincides with a surge in demand, fueled by the long-awaited approval of spot Bitcoin exchange-traded funds (ETFs) by regulators.

The advent of Bitcoin ETFs has opened the floodgates for institutional capital to flow into the crypto market. Wall Street titans like BlackRock and

Fidelity have seized the opportunity, launching their own Bitcoin ETF products and snapping up a significant portion of the available supply. This institutionalization of crypto has lent credibility to the asset class and catalyzed a wave of demand from investors seeking exposure to this burgeoning market.

Data from crypto investment product providers paints a picture of unprecedented inflows. In a single week, digital investment products witnessed the second-highest weekly inflows on record, totaling a staggering $1.84 billion, with an overwhelming 94% of those inflows directed towards Bitcoin products. Trading volumes in these products soared to record levels, further underscoring the insatiable appetite for crypto exposure.

While high interest rates have traditionally been perceived as a headwind for risky assets, the crypto market appears to be shrugging off this concern, at least for the time being. Market participants have taken solace in the fact that the threat of further aggressive rate hikes by central banks, particularly the Federal Reserve, has diminished, providing a respite from the relentless tightening cycle.

This temporary pause in rate hike expectations has offered a window of opportunity for crypto to shine as investors seek out alternative assets with the potential for outsized returns. The allure of crypto's decentralized nature, immune to the machinations of central banks and traditional financial institutions, has only grown stronger in an environment of heightened economic uncertainty.

As the crypto market basks in the glow of renewed optimism, analysts and industry experts have not shied away from making bold price predictions. Some prominent voices have forecasted that Bitcoin could reach dizzying heights of $200,000 or even $500,000 in the long run, driven by the supply-demand imbalance and the ever-increasing institutional adoption.

While these predictions may seem audacious, they underscore the growing belief that cryptocurrencies are no longer a fringe phenomenon but rather a legitimate asset class that is here to stay. As more institutional players enter the fray, the crypto market is poised to experience a level of maturity and mainstream acceptance that was once thought unimaginable.

Amid this backdrop of unprecedented demand and institutional embrace, it is crucial to examine the factors that have catalyzed this crypto renaissance. One key driver has been the regulatory approval of Bitcoin ETFs, which has opened the doors for institutional investors to gain exposure to the crypto market with relative ease.

For years, the lack of a regulated and accessible investment vehicle had been a significant barrier to entry for institutions seeking to venture into the crypto space. However, with the advent of Bitcoin ETFs, this hurdle has been removed, paving the way for a flood of institutional capital to enter the market.

Major asset managers, such as BlackRock and Fidelity, have seized this opportunity, recognizing the growing demand for crypto exposure among their clients. These firms have launched their own Bitcoin ETF products, providing a regulated and transparent avenue for investors to gain exposure to the cryptocurrency market.

The impact of this institutional adoption cannot be overstated. Not only does it bring a significant influx of capital into the market, but it also lends credibility and mainstream acceptance to cryptocurrencies. As more reputable financial institutions embrace crypto, it becomes increasingly difficult to dismiss it as a mere speculative fad.

Moreover, the supply-demand dynamics underpinning the crypto market have created a perfect storm for price appreciation. The impending Bitcoin halving event, which occurs every four years, is set to reduce the rate at which new bitcoins enter the market by half. This supply squeeze comes at a time when demand is surging, driven by the influx of institutional capital and the growing recognition of crypto as a legitimate asset class.

The combination of these factors has resulted in a supply-demand imbalance that has tilted the scales in favor of higher prices. As more investors clamor for exposure to Bitcoin and other cryptocurrencies, the limited supply becomes increasingly valuable, fueling a self-reinforcing cycle of price appreciation.

While the crypto market's resilience amid high interest rates has been remarkable, it is important to note that this phenomenon is not without its risks and challenges. The crypto ecosystem remains highly volatile, and the potential for sharp price fluctuations remains a constant threat.

Furthermore, the regulatory landscape surrounding cryptocurrencies is still evolving, and the possibility of increased scrutiny or stricter regulations cannot be discounted. As more institutional players enter the market, there may be calls for tighter oversight and governance, which could impact the decentralized nature of cryptocurrencies.

Despite these challenges, the crypto market has demonstrated an uncanny ability to thrive in the face of adversity. As the world grapples with the complexities of a high-interest rate environment, the crypto revolution continues to unfold, rewriting the rules of finance and ushering in a new era of decentralized, democratized investing.

As investors and market participants navigate this uncharted territory, it is clear that the crypto market has emerged as a force to be reckoned with, defying conventional wisdom and capturing the imaginations of investors across the globe. While the road ahead is likely to be paved with challenges and volatility, the resurgence of crypto amid high interest rates serves as a testament to the resilience and adaptability of this burgeoning asset class.

Chapter 2: Drivers of the Crypto Rally

The recent surge in cryptocurrency prices, particularly Bitcoin's ascent towards its all-time highs, has been fueled by a confluence of factors that have created a perfect storm for bullish sentiment in the market. These drivers have not only defied conventional wisdom but also showcased the unique dynamics that govern the crypto ecosystem. In this chapter, we will delve into the key catalysts propelling this remarkable rally.

At the heart of the crypto rally lies a fundamental supply-demand imbalance that has tilted the scales in favor of higher prices. This imbalance has been exacerbated by two interrelated factors: the impending Bitcoin halving event and the rising institutional demand for cryptocurrencies.

Bitcoin, the pioneering and most widely recognized cryptocurrency, is designed with a built-in mechanism that periodically reduces the rate at which new bitcoins are introduced into circulation. This event, known as the "halving," occurs approximately every four years and is a critical aspect of Bitcoin's underlying protocol.

During the halving, the reward for mining new blocks on the Bitcoin blockchain is cut in half, effectively reducing the supply of new bitcoins entering the market. This built-in scarcity is a fundamental feature of Bitcoin's design and is intended to maintain its long-term value proposition as a deflationary asset.

The upcoming halving event, scheduled for 2024, has generated significant anticipation and speculation within the crypto community. Historical data from previous halvings suggests that these events have often been followed by substantial price rallies, as the reduced supply fails to keep pace with the increasing demand.

In the 12 months following the 2020 halving, Bitcoin's price surged by a staggering 8,069%, while the 2016 and 2012 halvings saw price increases of 284% and 559%, respectively. These remarkable gains highlight the potential impact of the supply squeeze on Bitcoin's valuation.

Coinciding with the impending halving event is a surge in institutional demand for cryptocurrencies, particularly Bitcoin. As the crypto market matures and gains mainstream recognition, an increasing number of institutional investors, asset managers, and financial institutions have been seeking exposure to this burgeoning asset class.

The entry of institutional players into the crypto market has been driven by a variety of factors, including the growing acceptance of cryptocurrencies as a legitimate investment vehicle, the potential for portfolio diversification, and the desire to capitalize on the market's growth potential.

Institutions have recognized the unique characteristics of cryptocurrencies, such as their decentralized nature, limited supply, and potential for global adoption, making them an attractive addition to investment portfolios. Furthermore, the increasing regulatory clarity surrounding cryptocurrencies has helped alleviate some of the concerns that previously deterred institutional participation.

This influx of institutional capital has created a significant demand-side pressure, as these deep-pocketed investors seek to accumulate substantial holdings in cryptocurrencies like Bitcoin. With limited supply and a finite number of bitcoins in circulation, this heightened demand has contributed to the upward price momentum witnessed in the market.

One of the most significant drivers of the crypto rally has been the emergence of Bitcoin exchange-traded funds (ETFs). The approval and subsequent launch of these regulated investment vehicles have opened the floodgates for institutional capital to flow into the crypto market with relative ease.

For years, the lack of a regulated and accessible investment vehicle had been a significant barrier to entry for institutions seeking to venture into the crypto space. However, the recent regulatory approvals of Bitcoin ETFs by various financial authorities have paved the way for a more mainstream adoption of cryptocurrencies.

These approvals have not only lent credibility to the crypto market but have also provided a level of oversight and transparency that has been welcomed by institutional investors. By adhering to stringent regulatory requirements, Bitcoin ETFs offer a regulated and compliant avenue for institutions to gain exposure to the crypto market.

The approval of Bitcoin ETFs has catalyzed a wave of institutional adoption, as major asset managers and financial institutions have seized the opportunity to launch their own crypto-focused investment products. Wall Street titans like BlackRock and Fidelity have been at the forefront of this movement, recognizing the growing demand for crypto exposure among their clients.

These institutions have launched their own Bitcoin ETF products, providing investors with a regulated and transparent way to gain exposure to the cryptocurrency market. By leveraging their extensive distribution networks and client bases, these asset managers have facilitated the influx of institutional capital into the crypto ecosystem.

The impact of this institutional adoption cannot be overstated. Not only does it bring a significant influx of capital into the market, but it also lends credibility and mainstream acceptance to cryptocurrencies. As more reputable financial institutions embrace crypto, it becomes increasingly difficult to dismiss it as a mere speculative fad.

The surge in institutional demand for cryptocurrencies has been reflected in the record-breaking inflows witnessed by crypto investment products. Data from providers of these products paint a picture of unprecedented appetite for crypto exposure.

In a single week, digital investment products witnessed the second-highest weekly inflows on record, totaling a staggering $1.84 billion. Remarkably, an overwhelming 94% of these inflows were directed towards Bitcoin products, underscoring the enduring dominance of the world's largest cryptocurrency.

Trading volumes in these investment products have also soared to record levels, further reinforcing the insatiable appetite for crypto exposure among institutional and retail investors alike. As more capital flows into these products, it creates a self-reinforcing cycle of demand, driving prices higher and attracting even more investment.

The magnitude of these inflows highlights the growing acceptance of cryptocurrencies as a legitimate investment asset class. As investors seek to diversify their portfolios and capitalize on the growth potential of the crypto market, these investment products have become a crucial gateway for gaining exposure.

While high interest rates have traditionally been perceived as a headwind for risk assets like cryptocurrencies, the recent crypto rally has shrugged off this concern, at least for the time being. Market participants have taken solace in the fact that the threat of further aggressive rate hikes by central banks, particularly the Federal Reserve, has diminished, providing a respite from the relentless tightening cycle.

This temporary pause in rate hike expectations has offered a window of opportunity for crypto to shine, as investors seek out alternative assets with the potential for outsized returns. The allure of crypto's decentralized nature, immune to the machinations of central banks and traditional financial institutions, has only grown stronger in an environment of heightened economic uncertainty.

As the fears surrounding aggressive rate hikes have subsided, at least temporarily, investors have been emboldened to allocate capital towards riskier assets like cryptocurrencies. The perceived reduction in monetary policy risks has contributed to the bullish sentiment driving the crypto rally.

However, it is important to note that the relationship between interest rates and crypto prices is complex and multifaceted. While easing rate hike concerns have provided a tailwind for the current rally, the long-term impact of sustained high interest rates on the crypto market remains uncertain and subject to ongoing debate within the investment community.

The drivers of the crypto rally have been diverse and multifaceted, showcasing the unique dynamics that govern this burgeoning asset class. The supply-demand imbalance, fueled by the impending Bitcoin halving and rising institutional demand, has created a powerful upward price momentum. The emergence of Bitcoin ETFs and their subsequent institutional adoption have unleashed a torrent of capital into the crypto market, further amplifying the rally. Record-breaking inflows into crypto investment products and easing rate hike concerns have added fuel to the fire, propelling cryptocurrencies to new heights.

As the crypto market continues to evolve and mature, these drivers are likely to shape its trajectory, presenting both opportunities and challenges for investors navigating this uncharted territory. While the future remains uncertain, one thing is clear: the crypto revolution has well and truly arrived, disrupting traditional finance and captivating the imaginations of investors worldwide.

Chapter 3: Institutional Embrace of Cryptocurrencies

The recent surge in cryptocurrency prices has been inextricably linked to the growing institutional embrace of this once-niche asset class. As the crypto market matures and gains mainstream recognition, an increasing number of institutional investors, asset managers, and financial institutions have been seeking exposure to this burgeoning ecosystem. This chapter will explore the pivotal role played by institutional adoption in driving the crypto rally and the significant impact of the emergence of Bitcoin exchange-traded funds (ETFs).

One of the most significant developments fueling the institutional embrace of cryptocurrencies has been the entry of major asset managers into the fray. These financial giants, with their vast resources and extensive client bases, have recognized the growing demand for crypto exposure and have taken decisive steps to capitalize on this opportunity.

Wall Street titans like BlackRock and Fidelity have been at the forefront of this movement, recognizing the potential of cryptocurrencies to disrupt traditional finance and offer their clients access to a new frontier of investing. These firms, once known for their cautious approach to emerging asset classes, have now become pioneers in the crypto space, launching their own Bitcoin ETF products and actively promoting their crypto offerings.

The decision by these industry heavyweights to venture into the crypto realm has been driven by a multitude of factors. Firstly, the growing acceptance of cryptocurrencies as a legitimate investment vehicle has prompted asset managers to reassess their stance on this asset class. As more institutional investors express interest in gaining exposure to crypto, these firms have been compelled to meet this demand to remain competitive and retain their client base.

Secondly, the potential for portfolio diversification and uncorrelated returns has been a compelling proposition for asset managers seeking to enhance their investment offerings. Cryptocurrencies, with their unique characteristics and limited correlation to traditional asset classes, offer the promise of diversification benefits and the potential to generate outsized returns.

Furthermore, the increasing regulatory clarity surrounding cryptocurrencies has helped alleviate some of the concerns that previously deterred institutional participation. As financial authorities around the world have taken steps to establish regulatory frameworks for the crypto market, asset managers have gained greater confidence in navigating this emerging landscape.

The entry of major asset managers into the crypto space has been a game-changer, catalyzing a wave of institutional adoption and lending credibility to the asset class. These firms, with their deep pockets and extensive distribution networks, have the potential to unleash a torrent of capital into the crypto market, driving prices higher and further fueling the ongoing rally.

One of the most significant catalysts for institutional adoption of cryptocurrencies has been the emergence of Bitcoin exchange-traded funds (ETFs). The approval and subsequent launch of these regulated investment vehicles have opened the floodgates for institutional capital to flow into the crypto market with relative ease.

For years, the lack of a regulated and accessible investment vehicle had been a significant barrier to entry for institutions seeking to venture into the crypto space. Traditional investment funds and asset managers were hesitant to delve into the crypto market due to concerns over regulatory uncertainty, custody challenges, and the perceived risks associated with direct investment in cryptocurrencies.

However, the recent regulatory approvals of Bitcoin ETFs by various financial authorities have paved the way for a more mainstream adoption of cryptocurrencies by institutional investors. These ETFs, which track the performance of Bitcoin, offer a regulated and compliant avenue for institutions to gain exposure to the crypto market while adhering to stringent regulatory requirements.

The impact of Bitcoin ETFs on institutional adoption cannot be overstated. By providing a regulated and transparent investment vehicle, these ETFs have effectively democratized access to the crypto market for a broader range of institutional investors. Asset managers, pension funds, and other institutional players can now seamlessly incorporate Bitcoin exposure into their portfolios, without the complexities associated with direct ownership and custody of cryptocurrencies.

Moreover, the launch of Bitcoin ETFs has catalyzed a wave of product innovation within the asset management industry. Major financial institutions, recognizing the potential for growth in the crypto space, have been quick to develop and market their own Bitcoin ETF offerings, competing for a share of the burgeoning institutional demand.

The influx of institutional capital facilitated by Bitcoin ETFs has had a profound impact on the crypto market. Not only does it bring a significant influx of new capital, but it also lends credibility and mainstream acceptance to cryptocurrencies. As more reputable financial institutions embrace crypto through regulated investment vehicles, it becomes increasingly difficult to dismiss the asset class as a mere speculative fad.

Furthermore, the presence of institutional investors in the crypto market has the potential to enhance liquidity and reduce volatility over time. As these deep-pocketed investors enter the fray, their substantial capital reserves and sophisticated trading strategies can help absorb market swings and provide a stabilizing force within the ecosystem.

However, it is important to note that the institutional embrace of cryptocurrencies is not without its challenges and potential risks. As more institutional players enter the market, there may be calls for increased regulation and oversight, which could potentially erode some of the decentralized nature that has been a defining characteristic of cryptocurrencies.

Additionally, the concentration of ownership among a few large institutional players raises concerns about the potential for market manipulation and the erosion of the democratized ethos that initially underpinned the crypto movement.

Nonetheless, the institutional embrace of cryptocurrencies, catalyzed by the emergence of Bitcoin ETFs, has been a pivotal development in the ongoing crypto rally. As more institutional capital flows into the market, it not only drives prices higher but also lends legitimacy and mainstream acceptance to this burgeoning asset class. The entry of major asset managers and the launch of regulated investment vehicles have ushered in a new era of institutional adoption, paving the way for the crypto market to reach new heights and further solidify its position within the global financial landscape.

Chapter 4: Supply Squeeze And Price Predictions

As the crypto market continues to defy expectations and challenge conventional wisdom, the stage is set for a potentially historic supply squeeze that could propel prices to unprecedented levels. This chapter delves into the highly anticipated Bitcoin halving event, its impact on supply dynamics, and the bold price predictions that have captivated the investment community.

At the core of Bitcoin's design lies an ingenious mechanism that ensures its long-term scarcity and value proposition – the halving event. This programmed occurrence, which takes place approximately every four years, is a defining feature of the world's largest cryptocurrency and has significant implications for its supply dynamics.

The Bitcoin halving is a pre-coded event that reduces the reward for mining new blocks on the

Bitcoin blockchain by half. This means that the rate at which new bitcoins enter circulation is effectively cut in half, resulting in a significant supply reduction.

The upcoming halving, scheduled for 2024, has generated immense anticipation and speculation within the crypto community. Market participants and analysts are closely monitoring this event, as historical data suggests that previous halvings have often been followed by substantial price rallies.

The rationale behind this price appreciation lies in the fundamental principles of supply and demand. As the supply of new bitcoins entering the market diminishes, while demand remains constant or increases, the existing supply becomes increasingly scarce, driving up its perceived value.

This supply squeeze is particularly significant in the context of the current crypto market landscape. The recent surge in institutional demand, fueled by the approval of Bitcoin ETFs and the entry of major asset managers, has created a powerful demand-side pressure. With deep-pocketed investors clamoring for exposure to Bitcoin, the limited supply resulting from the halving event could potentially trigger a supply-demand imbalance of epic proportions.

Moreover, the halving event holds symbolic significance within the crypto community, often serving as a catalyst for renewed interest and speculation. As the event approaches, heightened media attention and investor focus could further amplify the demand for Bitcoin, contributing to a self-reinforcing cycle of price appreciation.

Amid the anticipation surrounding the impending Bitcoin halving and the supply squeeze it promises, analysts and industry experts have not shied away from making bold price predictions. These forecasts, which may seem audacious to some, underscore the growing belief that cryptocurrencies are no longer a fringe phenomenon but rather a legitimate asset class poised for mainstream adoption.

One of the most widely discussed price targets for Bitcoin is the $200,000 mark, a level that would represent a significant milestone in the cryptocurrency's journey. Prominent voices in the industry, including Standard Chartered, have predicted that the combination of the Bitcoin halving and the influx of institutional capital through ETFs could propel prices to this lofty level.

Standard Chartered's analysts have cited the supply-demand dynamics as a key driver for their bullish prediction. They argue that the finite supply of Bitcoin, coupled with the surging demand from institutional investors and the constraints imposed by the halving event, could create a perfect storm for price appreciation.

Moreover, the growing acceptance of Bitcoin as a legitimate store of value and hedge against inflation has bolstered the case for higher price targets. As more investors seek to diversify their portfolios and protect their wealth from the eroding effects of fiat currency debasement, Bitcoin's perceived scarcity and limited supply could make it an increasingly attractive investment proposition.

While the $200,000 price target may seem ambitious, some analysts have ventured even further, suggesting that Bitcoin could ultimately reach the dizzying heights of $500,000 or more. This bold prediction has been put forth by Tom Lee, the co-founder and head of research at Fundstrat Global Advisors.

Lee's bullish outlook is predicated on the belief that the crypto market is still in its infancy and that the widespread adoption of Bitcoin as a mainstream asset is inevitable. He argues that the influx of institutional capital facilitated by ETFs and the growing recognition of Bitcoin's scarcity and utility will drive demand to unprecedented levels.

"There's a finite supply and now we have a potentially huge increase in demand with spot bitcoin ETF approval," Lee explained in a recent interview. "So I think in five years something around half a million would be potentially achievable."

Lee's prediction is rooted in the idea that as more institutional investors allocate a portion of their portfolios to Bitcoin, the limited supply will become increasingly valuable, fueling a self-reinforcing cycle of price appreciation.

Furthermore, Lee and other proponents of this lofty price target point to the potential for Bitcoin to disrupt and eventually replace traditional fiat currencies as a global reserve asset. If Bitcoin were to achieve this level of adoption and utility, its scarcity and decentralized nature could make it a highly sought-after asset, driving prices to levels that may seem inconceivable today.

While these price predictions may seem audacious to some, they underscore the growing belief that cryptocurrencies, and Bitcoin in particular, are on the cusp of a transformative shift. As more institutional players enter the fray, and the supply-demand dynamics tilt further in favor of scarcity, the stage is set for a potentially historic price rally that could redefine the boundaries of the crypto market.

However, it is important to note that these predictions are inherently speculative and subject to numerous variables and uncertainties. The crypto market remains highly volatile, and unforeseen events or regulatory shifts could significantly impact price trajectories. Additionally, the adoption of cryptocurrencies as mainstream assets is still in its early stages, and the path to widespread acceptance may be fraught with challenges and obstacles.

Nonetheless, the supply squeeze promised by the upcoming Bitcoin halving, coupled with the institutional embrace and bold price predictions, has created a perfect storm of bullish sentiment in the crypto market. As investors and market participants navigate this uncharted territory, one thing is certain: the crypto revolution is far from over, and its potential to disrupt traditional finance and reshape the global financial landscape remains an enticing prospect for those willing to embrace its volatility and uncertainty.

Chapter 5: Navigating the Crypto Bull Run

As the crypto market continues to defy expectations and capture the attention of investors worldwide, navigating the ongoing bull run requires a careful balance of seizing opportunities and mitigating risks. This chapter will explore the potential prospects and pitfalls that lie ahead, as well as the evolving regulatory landscape and strategies for prudent investment in this dynamic and volatile asset class.

The crypto bull run presents a unique set of opportunities and risks that investors must carefully consider before committing capital to this burgeoning market. On the one hand, the potential for outsized returns and the diversification benefits offered by cryptocurrencies make them an enticing prospect. However, the inherent volatility and uncertainties surrounding this asset class demand a cautious and well-informed approach.

One of the primary opportunities presented by the crypto bull run lies in the potential for capital appreciation. As institutional adoption accelerates and the supply-demand dynamics tilt in favor of scarcity, cryptocurrencies like Bitcoin could experience significant price gains. This prospect has already fueled bold price predictions from analysts, with some forecasting Bitcoin reaching dizzying heights of $200,000 or even $500,000 in the long run.

Additionally, the decentralized nature of cryptocurrencies and their potential to disrupt traditional financial systems offer investors a unique opportunity to participate in a technological revolution. As more industries and use cases emerge for blockchain technology and digital assets, early adopters and forward-thinking investors could reap substantial rewards.

However, the crypto market is not without its risks. Volatility remains a defining characteristic of this asset class, with prices prone to sudden and dramatic swings. This volatility can be exacerbated by speculative trading, regulatory uncertainties, and the inherent risks associated with emerging technologies.

Furthermore, the crypto ecosystem is still relatively nascent, and the long-term viability and adoption of many cryptocurrencies remain uncertain. Investors must exercise caution and conduct thorough due diligence to avoid falling victim to potential scams, pump-and-dump schemes, or projects with questionable fundamentals.

Cybersecurity risks also loom large, as the digital nature of cryptocurrencies makes them vulnerable to hacking attempts, theft, and other malicious activities. Investors must take proactive measures to secure their digital assets and ensure the safety of their investments.

The regulatory landscape surrounding cryptocurrencies remains a pivotal factor in shaping the trajectory of the crypto bull run. As more institutional players enter the market and mainstream adoption accelerates, regulatory authorities around the world are grappling with the challenge of establishing clear and consistent frameworks for the governance of digital assets.

In recent years, there has been a noticeable shift towards greater regulatory clarity and acceptance of cryptocurrencies by various jurisdictions. The approval of Bitcoin ETFs by financial regulators, for instance, has been a game-changer, opening the doors for institutional capital to flow into the crypto market with relative ease.

However, the regulatory landscape remains fragmented, with different countries and regions adopting varying approaches to crypto regulation. Some nations have embraced a more welcoming stance, recognizing the potential of blockchain technology and digital assets, while others have taken a more cautious or outright hostile approach, citing concerns over financial stability, investor protection, and the potential for illicit activities.

As the crypto market continues to evolve, investors must remain vigilant and stay abreast of the ever-changing regulatory landscape. Shifts in regulatory policies, whether at the national or international level, can have profound implications for the crypto ecosystem, influencing everything from market sentiment and liquidity to compliance requirements and taxation.

Moreover, the increasing institutional presence in the crypto market may prompt calls for more robust regulation and oversight. While this could bring about greater stability and legitimacy for the asset class, it also raises concerns about the potential erosion of the decentralized ethos that initially underpinned the crypto movement.

Given the unique characteristics and risks associated with the crypto market, investors must carefully consider their investment strategies and risk management approaches. While there is no one-size-fits-all solution, several prudent strategies have emerged as the crypto bull run continues to unfold.

Diversification remains a crucial tenet of sound investment strategy, even within the crypto realm. While Bitcoin and other major cryptocurrencies may dominate the headlines, investors should consider allocating a portion of their portfolios to a diverse range of digital assets, including altcoins and emerging projects with promising use cases and fundamentals.

Dollar-cost averaging, a strategy that involves investing a fixed amount at regular intervals, can help mitigate the impact of volatility and reduce the risk of poorly timed entries or exits. By spreading out investments over time, investors can potentially benefit from both upswings and downturns in the market.

For investors with a higher risk tolerance and a longer-term investment horizon, the concept of "HODLing" (holding on for dear life) may be an appropriate strategy. This approach involves buying and holding cryptocurrencies through market cycles, with the belief that the long-term upward trajectory will eventually outweigh short-term fluctuations.

Risk management is paramount in the crypto market, and investors should consider implementing stop-loss orders, position sizing, and other risk-mitigation techniques to protect their capital. Additionally, the use of cold wallets and hardware wallets for securely storing digital assets can help mitigate the risk of cyber attacks and theft.

Furthermore, investors should remain vigilant and conduct thorough research before committing capital to any crypto project or investment opportunity. Due diligence is essential in separating legitimate ventures from potential scams or projects with questionable fundamentals.

Lastly, investors should stay informed and engaged with the crypto community, as this rapidly evolving market is often driven by sentiment, news, and emerging trends. Keeping abreast of developments in the regulatory landscape, technological advancements, and market dynamics can help investors make informed decisions and seize opportunities as they arise.

In conclusion, navigating the crypto bull run requires a delicate balance of prudence and opportunism. While the potential rewards are enticing, the inherent risks and volatility of the crypto market demand a well-informed and disciplined approach to investing. By understanding the opportunities and risks, staying abreast of the regulatory landscape, and adopting sound investment strategies, investors can position themselves to potentially capitalize on the ongoing crypto revolution while mitigating the associated risks.

Conclusion

The recent crypto bull run has been nothing short of remarkable, defying conventional wisdom and challenging long-held assumptions about the interplay between risk assets and macroeconomic conditions. As central banks around the world grappled with soaring inflation and implemented aggressive monetary tightening measures, the crypto market has displayed an uncanny resilience, shrugging off the headwinds of high interest rates and staging a remarkable comeback.

Throughout this period of economic uncertainty and policy shifts, cryptocurrencies, led by the pioneering Bitcoin, have not only held their ground but have surged to unprecedented heights, inching closer to their all-time highs and captivating the attention of investors worldwide. This resilience has been fueled by a potent cocktail of supply-demand dynamics, institutional adoption, and a growing recognition of the intrinsic value proposition offered by digital assets.

At the heart of this crypto renaissance lies the impending Bitcoin halving event, a programmed occurrence that will reduce the rate at which new bitcoins enter circulation by half. This supply squeeze, coinciding with a surge in institutional demand driven by the advent of regulated Bitcoin ETFs, has created a powerful upward price momentum that has defied conventional economic theory.

As major asset managers and financial institutions have flocked to the crypto market, seeking exposure to this burgeoning asset class, they have unleashed a torrent of capital that has further amplified the rally. Record-breaking inflows into crypto investment products and soaring trading volumes have underscored the insatiable appetite for digital assets among both institutional and retail investors.

Moreover, the temporary pause in aggressive rate hike expectations has provided a respite for risk assets, allowing the allure of crypto's decentralized nature and potential for outsized returns to shine through. As investors seek alternative investment avenues amid heightened economic uncertainty, the crypto market has emerged as an enticing proposition, immune to the machinations of central banks and traditional financial institutions.

This resilience in the face of macroeconomic headwinds has not gone unnoticed by analysts and industry experts, who have not shied away from making bold price predictions. Forecasts of Bitcoin reaching dizzying heights of $200,000 or even $500,000 in the long run have captured the imagination of investors, fueling further speculation and excitement within the crypto community.

While these predictions may seem audacious to some, they underscore the growing belief that cryptocurrencies are no longer a fringe phenomenon but rather a legitimate asset class poised for mainstream adoption. As more institutional players enter the fray and the supply-demand dynamics tilt further in favor of scarcity, the stage is set for a potentially historic price rally that could redefine the boundaries of the crypto market.

As the crypto market basks in the glow of renewed optimism and robust institutional embrace, it is crucial to consider the future outlook and potential trajectories that lie ahead. While the road ahead is likely to be paved with challenges and volatility, the crypto revolution has demonstrated an uncanny ability to thrive in the face of adversity, constantly evolving and adapting to new realities.

One of the key factors that will shape the future of the crypto market is the evolving regulatory landscape. As more institutional players enter the fray and mainstream adoption accelerates, there will likely be calls for increased regulation and oversight. While this could bring about greater stability and legitimacy for the asset class, it also raises concerns about the potential erosion of the decentralized ethos that initially underpinned the crypto movement.

Striking the right balance between regulation and preserving the core principles of decentralization and transparency will be a delicate dance for regulators and industry stakeholders. Overregulation could stifle innovation and erode the very qualities that make cryptocurrencies appealing, while a lack of clear and consistent frameworks could hinder mainstream adoption and deter institutional investors.

Additionally, the future outlook of the crypto market will be heavily influenced by the pace of technological innovation and the emergence of new use cases for blockchain technology and digital assets. As more industries explore the potential applications of this disruptive technology, new opportunities for growth and value creation may arise, further fueling the demand for cryptocurrencies.

The development of scalability solutions, enhanced security protocols, and user-friendly interfaces could also play a pivotal role in driving mass adoption. As the crypto ecosystem becomes more accessible and user-friendly, it could attract a broader range of investors and participants, further solidifying its position as a mainstream financial instrument.

Furthermore, the future trajectory of the crypto market will be shaped by the interplay between supply and demand dynamics. While the upcoming Bitcoin halving event promises a supply squeeze, the long-term sustainability of price appreciation will hinge on the ability of demand to keep pace with the limited supply. Continued institutional adoption, coupled with the emergence of new use cases and real-world applications, could fuel sustained demand and drive prices higher.

However, it is important to note that the crypto market remains highly volatile and susceptible to speculative forces. Sudden shifts in market sentiment, regulatory crackdowns, or technological disruptions could trigger dramatic price swings and periods of turbulence. Investors must remain vigilant and prepared to navigate these uncertainties, employing sound risk management strategies and maintaining a long-term perspective.

As the crypto revolution continues to unfold, one thing is certain: the future of finance is being rewritten before our very eyes. The resilience and adaptability displayed by the crypto market in the face of macroeconomic headwinds have cemented its status as a force to be reckoned with, captivating the imaginations of investors and challenging the traditional paradigms of the financial world.

Whether cryptocurrencies ultimately realize their full potential as a disruptive force or settle into a more niche role within the broader financial ecosystem remains to be seen. However, the ongoing crypto bull run has served as a powerful testament to the enduring appeal of decentralization, transparency, and the pursuit of alternative investment avenues beyond the confines of traditional finance.

As we navigate the uncharted waters of this digital age, the crypto market will undoubtedly continue to evolve, presenting both opportunities and challenges for those brave enough to embrace its volatility and uncertainties. The future outlook may be shrouded in ambiguity, but one thing is certain: the crypto revolution has ignited a spark that cannot be easily extinguished, and its impact on the global financial landscape will be felt for generations to come.

www.ingramcontent.com/pod-product-compliance
Lightning Source LLC
Chambersburg PA
CBHW070218260726
48658CB00006BA/2111